ELECTION of VICAR for CLERKENWELL.

Address, Probationary Sermons,

Testimonials, &c.,

OF THE

REV. WILLIAM HOLDERNESS,

CANDIDATE.

AUGUST, 1875.

'UBLIC PRESS.

⸱

ıd *Telegraph*, founded upon an
f your behaviour at the Parish
ılıu see ne naü some grounu in tnat
nd been called to the parish. Would
ı a matter of prayer? He trusted
did, then those prayer meetings that
aturday night would not have been
ıd prolonged applause.)
the close of the proceedings, said the
ı had not received the official com-
to earlier was because the church-
n Mr. Maguire that they could take
lection until the living was actually
ə, and until they had received a com-
shop of London to that effect. They
s communication for some time, and
ɔ come, they waited upon him, and
waited a long time before they re-
MR. ROSE WAS IN THE
SET ABOUT HIS CAN-
ONCE, and Mr. Holderness
of coming into the field earlier
ɔandidates, through having friends in
both these gentlemen would have
me footing as the other candidates.
ɘns) had endeavoured to show the
the election, and would also endeav-
re. (Hear, hear, and applause.)"

Un ——————

s who it is that at-
ıg your proceedings.

ELECTION FOR VICAR, AND THE PUBLIC PRESS.

FELLOW PARISHIONERS OF CLERKENWELL,

Have you read the quotations from the articles of the *Standard* and *Telegraph*, founded upon an infamous, scurilous, and lying account, of Mr. HOLDERNESS' speech, and of your behaviour at the Parish Meeting of the 11th inst.

There cannot be a doubt this report was made, or paid for, by the gentlemen who now, coward like, seek to shelter themselves behind the *we* of pretended impartial journalism, for the purpose of instilling into a cause venom they dare not openly use.

· If you have read the remarks referred to, examine also their antidote, as follows, copied from your own Local and Independent Organ, the *Clerkenwell News* of August 13th, whose Editor knows the facts.

EXTRACTS.

" A meeting of the parishioners of Clerkenwell was held in the Amwell-street School-room, on Wednesday evening, for the purpose of hearing addresses from the candidates for the vacant living of the Parish. The chair was taken by Churchwarden Culver, who was supported by the other churchwarden, Mr. Goad. The meeting, which had been called by requisition from several parishioners, was of course a crowded one, BUT A VERY ATTENTIVE HEARING was given to each of the three candidates who delivered addresses.

The Rev. W. HOLDERNESS, who was received with loud applause, several times renewed, said he could not help thinking that evening what all this commotion was about. They were only going to select guide posts that would point them continually to the land of God—clergymen were, so to speak, only sign posts that must keep pointing, pointing, pointing heavenward. (Applause.) In the North of England, instead of painting directions in black or white letters on the finger-posts by the road-side, they, in some cases, cut the letters through the direction board, so that on a moonlight or starlight night the names of the places could be plainly deciphered, and so they as clergymen and ministerial direction posts had no power in themselves to direct them from this dark land to the eternal one excepting by the light of heaven shining through them, and showing them the way to God. (Applause.) He was not going to speak to them for himself that evening, but for the Rev William Holderness, vicar of Woolfardisworthy West. He was going to speak as if that reverend gentleman was his client, for he had too much modesty to speak of himself. (Laughter.) A great deal of the unpleasantness and commotion at these elections could be avoided if they steered clear of personalities, and confined themselves to the broad principles and real issues of the contest. They should not trouble what Dick said of Tom, or Tom said of Harry, and so on, but let all such quibbles take care of themselves, and straightway go and

the Rev. James Holderness (the speaker's brother), curate number three, and curate number four, the Rev. Mr Spurgeon,

or any other excellent minister.

(Applause.) He said that number of curates advisedly, because it had been said Mr. Spurgeon did a great work in training young men for the Ministry, and so if they would give him curates enough he would go on training young men for the ministry as he had hitherto. The Church wanted it. Some of his opponents had tried to pick little holes in his testimonials, and the result was that he had been induced to obtain others of ten times greater weight. Then, again, one of the dear friends had said he was always in Mr. Clutterbuck's church. He didn't know Mr. Clutterbuck, but he told them this, that the NUNNERY NEAR HIS LODGINGS would get the smallest assistance from him if he came into the parish, nor did he think it had received any from Mr. Maguire. His object, if he came to Clerkenwell, would be to set forth Christ and Him crucified, and to have no APEING OF ROME whatever (Applause.) Many people had told him that if they knew him at the first they would have done so-and-so. There would be no occassion to disturb a single official in the church if he came there; there would be no occasion to lose Mr. Maguire or their truly-beloved friend Mr. Rose, and there would be no occasion to lose Mr Ough. There by requisition from several parishioners, was of course a crowded one, BUT A VERY ATTENTIVE HEARING was given to each of the three candidates who delivered addresses.

The Rev. W. HOLDERNESS, who was received with loud applause, several times renewed, said he could not help thinking that evening what all this commotion was about. They were only going to select guide posts that would point them continually to the land of God—clergymen were, so to speak, only sign posts that must keep pointing, pointing, pointing heavenward. (Applause.) In the North of England, instead of painting directions in black or white letters on the finger-posts by the road-side, they, in some cases, cut the letters through the direction board, so that on a moonlight or starlight night the names of the places could be plainly deciphered, and so they as clergymen and ministerial direction posts had no power in themselves to direct them from this dark land to the eternal one excepting by the light of heaven shining through them, and showing them the way to God. (Applause.) He was not going to speak to them for himself that evening, but for the Rev William Holderness, vicar of Woolfardisworthy West. He was going to speak as if that reverend gentleman was his client, for he had too much modesty to speak of himself. (Laughter.) A great deal of the unpleasantness and commotion at these elections could be avoided if they steered clear of personalities, and confined themselves to the broad principles and real issues of the contest. They should not trouble what Dick said of Tom, or Tom said of Harry, and so on, but let all such quibbles take care of themselves, and straightway go and ascertain what sort of a man they wanted for vicar of the parish, and which was the most suitable candidate for the post in the field. (Renewed applause.) The idea that prevailed when he first came among them that it was very wrong and un-Christian to come to Clerkenwell and oppose Mr. Rose had now been given up, and Mr. ROSE had himself told them very properly that the field WAS OPEN TO ALL ENGLAND Some of his opponents had made it a point that he had stated he should continue to contest the election if angels or archangels came into the field, forgetting that the commission to preach the Gospel was given to man, and never to angels. This was not his own idea, but Molyneux's, who used to say. "I would not change places with an angel." Why? "Because to us men is given the commission to preach the Gospel." He did not then think it was at all un-Christian for him to come into this contest, seeing that it was open to all England and to all Ireland as well. It was the United Church of England and Ireland, and he believed that a gentleman from Dublin would not be disqualified as a candidate for that living by reason of his coming from Dublin or any other part of Ireland. (Laughter, and hear, hear.) He had spent his whole life in preparing for the ministry, and he believed he had spent it pretty well. No one would be more welcome to his pulpit, if he became vicar of Clerkenwell, than Mr. Maguire. He had done a great work in the parish, and well had their friend Mr. Rose eulogised him, but not more than he deserved, and therefore he should have his (Mr. Holderness's) pulpit as often as he liked to come to Clerkenwell to preach if he were elected. The first man he should ask to take the pulpit would be the Rev. Robert Maguire. Thus they would have Mr. Maguire, then would come Mr. Holderness, then Mr. Rose as curate number one, Mr. Ough as a curate number two, the Rev. James Holderness (the speaker's brother), curate number three, and curate number four, the Rev. Mr Spurgeon,

or any other excellent minister.

(Applause.) He said that number of curates advisedly, because it had been said Mr. Spurgeon did a great work in training young men for the Ministry, and so if they would give him curates enough he would go on training young men for the ministry as he had hitherto. The Church wanted it. Some of his opponents had tried to pick little holes in his testimonials, and the result was that he had been induced to obtain others of ten times greater weight. Then, again, one of the dear friends had said he was always in Mr. Clutterbuck's church. He didn't know Mr. Clutterbuck, but he told them this, that the NUNNERY NEAR HIS LODGINGS would get the smallest assistance from him if he came into the parish, nor did he think it had received any from Mr. Maguire. His object, if he came to Clerkenwell, would be to set forth Christ and Him crucified, and to have no APEING OF ROME whatever (Applause.) Many people had told him that if they knew him at the first they would have done so-and-so. There would be no occassion to disturb a single official in the church if he came there; there would be no occasion to lose Mr. Maguire or their truly-beloved friend Mr. Rose, and there would be no occasion to lose Mr. Ough. There would be no occasion for anyone to stir from his or her position at all; he did not come to scatter, but to bind together. (Applause.) Would they do in this matter as he had done? He was speaking now to men of prayer. He had made this a matter of earnest and serious prayer, and if he told them exactly the steps by which he happened to come before them as a candidate, they would see he had some ground in that al. ne for believing he had been called to the parish. Would they make this election a matter of prayer? He trusted they would, and if they did, then those prayer meetings that had been held every Saturday night would not have been held in vain. (Loud and prolonged applause.)

The CHAIRMAN, at the close of the proceedings, said the reason why Mr. Close had not received the official communication he referred to earlier was because the churchwardens understood from Mr. Maguire that they could take no official steps in the election until the living was actually vacated by Mr. Maguire, and until they had received a communication from the Bishop of London to that effect. They waited for the Bishop's communication for some time, and then, finding it did not come, they waited upon him, and found they might have waited a long time before they received it from him. MR. ROSE WAS IN THE PARISH, AND SET ABOUT HIS CANDIDATURE AT ONCE, and Mr. Holderness had the advantage of coming into the field earlier than some of the other candidates, through having friends in Clerkenwell, otherwise both these gentlemen would have been placed on the same footing as the other candidates. They the (churchwardens) had endeavoured to show the strictest impartiality in the election, and would also endeavour to do so in the future. (Hear, hear, and applause.)"

ELECTORS! Compare and judge for yourselves who it is that attempts to degrade your character by burlesquing your proceedings.

40, Wilmington Square,
Clerkenwell, London,
16th August, 1875.

TO THE

CHURCHWARDENS, VESTRYMEN, AND RATEPAYING ELECTORS

OF THE

VICAR OF CLERKENWELL.

Ladies and Gentlemen,—

My appearance amongst you as a Candidate was on this wise.

When Sunday Evening Lecturer at the Parish Church, Bideford, there was amongst that goodly congregation a Christian father and his family, who belonged to the Wesleyan body. The head of that house used to say, " *No man can draw me from the Chapel to the Church of England except Mr. Holderness.*"

It came to pass, that the requirements of business drew one of the sons (Mr. R. Squire) to Clerkenwell.

After a while, the vacancy in the Vicariate arose, through the promotion of the Rev. Robert Maguire, and the mind of Mr. Squire reverted at once to his late spiritual instructor, causing him to earnestly desire that the teeming *thousands* of Clerkenwell should enjoy those ministrations which the rural and provincial *hundreds* loved.

As the candidature is open to all PROTESTANT clergymen of the United Churches of England and Ireland, the moment

The rise of Candidature.

the resignation was made known to me, with its Providential guidings and surroundings, I wrote to the Churchwardens, through Mr. Maguire, stating my desire to be a Candidate.

The start. Believing that no one would stir until the 6th July, when Mr. Maguire's resignation would be officially declared, I remained quietly with "*my few sheep in the wilderness,*" until. to my surprise, I heard that very active measures indeed had been taken by the Curate-in-charge; that, in fact, before the starters had time to say "OFF," one competitor had bounded away and was well advanced to the goal.

Seeing how matters stood, I ran after the premature starter. with the intention of overtaking and passing him in the race.

First Meeting. With these designs, I attended our first meeting in the little upper room, Amwell Street, on Monday, the 28th June. At the time appointed, very few persons appeared, and they were cautiously reconnoitring the new comer, rather than rushing into his arms with kind enthusiasm. The cautious kindness of these eighteen or twenty gentlemen was more pleasing to me and creditable to themselves than any uninformed ardour could have been

First Formation of Committee. As I related to them the incidents connected with my appearance amongst them—the motives which brought me there, my principles as a Protestant English Clergyman. holding the Thirty-nine Articles in their natural sense, and the plans which I proposed to pursue—I saw, in their interested and animated countenances, and I heard, in the sympathetic words which burst from their lips, that I had already won not a little of their approbation.

A Central Committee was formed and the following manifesto drawn up :—

To the Churchwardens, Vestrymen, and Ratepayers—
Electors of the Vicar of Clerkenwell.

GENTLEMEN,—I am moved to ask permission to become a candidate for the pastorate of your important parish—

Because, 1st.—It is my belief that as my early clerical labours were upon your noble river, which is the very life's blood of your vast City—so am I impressed that the mission of my riper years and experience will be amongst your dense population.

Because, 2nd.—I deem we are bound to take the Gospel Message to the largest number of persons in the shortest period of time, seeing that life is short, and we are commanded "to go into all the world and preach the Gospel *to every creature,*" therefore I am constrained to enter the *widest effectual door* that is opened unto me.

Because, 3rd.—With the commission to preach the WORD, our Great Captain also gave *power* to deliver His message acceptably to the people, enabling me to *win* souls by PERSUADING men that the benevolent designs of the Heavenly Father were to make all His children superlatively happy through time and ETERNITY.

Because, 4th.—I am entirely free, from a shadow of a shade, of the slightest Ritualistic tendency, looking with deep sorrow upon the havoc which diluted Romanism has made in the Protestant Church, and in English homes, hearts, and parishes.

Because, 5th.—I am a man of business; a friend of organised division of labour, who would set every man, woman, and child to work by parochial machinery and voluntary effort, to relieve the vast amount of human misery at our very doors, and to evidence that our Christianity consisteth not in preaching and lecturing only, but in going also from house to house, DOING GOOD, after the example of our Great Teacher.

Because, 6th. I love and can work with all who love our Lord Jesus Christ, irrespective of party names and sects. My field is the parish, and my flock all the inhabitants thereof.

Because, 7th.—My aspirations for good government are in the main similar to those of the majority of the most thoughful and respectful inhabitants of Clerkenwell, and I take a great interest in their scientific and mechanical pursuits, remembering that our Lord was a carpenter, and that the Apostle of the Gentiles was in a double sense a *workman* that needed not to be ashamed of his productions.

Because, 8th.—Your parish swarms with children who require religious instruction in your Sunday Schools. This is a part of your Vicar's duty, which I much enjoy, and in which I have had long experience; always considering our blessed Lord's command to feed His lambs as imperative as His injunction to feed His sheep.

Because, lastly.—Those who know me best have always averred that I was adapted for the work I seek amongst a large population. I share this impression with my friends, and consequently have been impelled to come before you. If your minds are similarly disposed I shall be your Vicar; if not, I shall cheerfully bow to your decision.

Pardon me, gentlemen, for trespassing so long on your patience. I will say no more, but call the following witnesses.

Yours faithfully,

WM. HOLDERNESS,
Vicar of Woolfardisworthy West.

TESTIMONIALS

From the Committee of the Thames Church Mission, whose names are here inscribed.

Patron.

HIS GRACE THE ARCHBISHOP OF CANTERBURY.

Vice-Patrons.

THE RIGHT HON. AND RIGHT REV. THE LORD BISHOP OF LONDON.
THE RIGHT REV. THE LORD BISHOP OF WINCHESTER.
THE RIGHT REV. THE LORD BISHOP OF ROCHESTER.

President.

THE RIGHT HON. THE LORD MAYOR, Conservator of the River Thames.

Vice-Presidents.

SIR JOHN HENRY BELL, BART, Deputy Master of the Trinity House.
REAR-ADMIRAL EARL WALDEGRAVE, C.B.

Committee.

Edward Absalom, Esq.	Rear-Admiral Sir H. Hart, Kt.
J. W. Alexander, Esq.	Rear-Admiral Hawker.
W. D. Atwood, Esq.	John Gurney Hoare, Esq.
Joseph Bainbridge, Esq.	Rear-Admiral Hope, C.B.
Captain Henry Bonham Box.	Stephen Kennard, Esq.
R. C. L. Bevan, Esq.	Hedworth Lambton, Esq.
C. J. Bevan, Esq.	Capt. the Hon. F. Maude, R.N.
The Marquis of Blandford.	Octavius Ommanney, Esq.
Henry Blanshard, Esq.	Capt. Sir G. G. Otway, Bt., R.N.
John Bockett, Esq.	Lord Alfred Paget.
Sir Edward N. Buxton, Bart.	George Pearce, Esq.
Capt. Alfred Chapman,	Jonathan Rashleigh, Esq.
Lord Henry Cholmondeley.	Capt. F. R. Rowley, R.N.
Captain Stephenson Ellerby.	Joseph Somes, Esq.
Richard Green, Esq.	Capt. D. Warren.

The following Resolution of Testimony to the Rev. WILLIAM HOLDERNESS was unanimously carried :—

Resolved.—The Committee cannot but express their deep regret at losing the valuable services of one who has devoted himself to the duties of the Mission, and take this opportunity of expressing to him their sincere thanks, and the assurance of their earnest prayers, that in his new sphere of duty his heavenly Father may abundantly bless his labours, and make him instrumental in bringing souls to Christ, through the preaching of the Gospel, as they have reason to hope and believe he has done during the seven years he has laboured in the Lord's vineyard through the instrumentality of the Thames Church Mission.

HON. CAPTAIN MAUDE, R.N., in the Chair.

17th June, 1872.

From the REV. DR. COOK, *Incumbent of Holy Trinity, Swansea.*

December, 1872.

The Rev. W. HOLDERNESS has been intimately known to me for many years, and, whilst I regard him as a truly godly and Christian brother, I know him to be a most zealous Clergyman and very assiduous and efficient worker. He is an affectionate and earnest preacher, and a diligent and painstaking Pastor; and in his various spheres of duty his untiring efforts have been blessed and attended with much success. I feel sure he would be valued and useful in any sphere to which he might be appointed.

CHAS COOK,

Incumbent of Holy Trinity, Swansea.

From CHARLES MARSHALL, M.A., *Harpurhey Rectory, Manchester.*

December 17th, 1872.

TO THE RIGHT HONOURABLE THE LORD CHANCELLOR, &c. &c.

MY LORD,

The Rev. WILLIAM HOLDERNESS has been known to me twenty-two years. I had so high an opinion of Mr. HOLDERNESS that eighteen years ago, at my instance, the Committee of the Thames Church Mission appointed him their Chaplain, an important and responsible post, which he filled so well for several years that influential members of that Committee represented to Her Majesty's Government Mr. HOLDERNESS' peculiar fitness for a Prison Chaplaincy—Mr. HOLDERNESS was at Portland, then moved to Dartmoor, and retires on its dissolution or closing. Mr. HOLDERNESS has ever maintained the high opinion I formed of him. He is sound in doctrine, of an amiable and conciliatory disposition, a painstaking Clergyman, and would be beloved in any parish to which he had the Presentation.

I have the honour to subscribe myself,

Your Lordship's most obedient, humble Servant,

CHARLES MARSHALL, M.A.

From G. W. W. HENDERSON, *Chairman, Board of Directors, Convict Prisons.*

45, *Parliament Street, London,*
November 22nd, 1865.

This is to certify that the Rev. W. HOLDERNESS was appointed a Chaplain in the Convict Service in July, 1853, and continued to discharge the important duties which devolved upon him with zeal, diligence, and fidelity, until March, 1865, when he retired from the service on the abolition of his office— the Chaplaincy of Dartmoor Convict Prison.

G. W.W. HENDERSON,

Chairman, Board of Directors, Convict Prisons.

(Successor to the late Sir Joshua Jebb, who was Chairman to the Board when I was appointed Chaplain by Lord Palmerston.)

From the Rev. C. W. CLARK, *Rector of Bridestow, Devon.*

November 30th, 1865.

The Rev. W. HOLDERNESS has been Curate of the Parish of Bridestow and Somton, and has shown himself capable of attracting and pleasing a large congregation in a scattered parish. It appears to me that the sphere of action for which his talents are adapted would be an intelligent town population. His active habits and social inclinations would, I think, be likely to have a considerable influence for good amongst educated classes. His manners are conciliatory, and his facility of illustration in delivering lectures, as well as for extempore pulpit discourses, would be valuable in clerical work in a populous neighbourhood. In his religious views as a Member of the Church of England there is no tendency to ritual or æsthetic exaggeration. I shall be glad to learn that

Mr. HOLDERNESS has found a sphere where he can develop his power and act upon a suitable population who would appreciate and value his powers of mind and energy of character.

CHAS. W. CLARKE,
Rector of Bridestow and Somton, Devonshire.

From the Rev. C. BARING GOULD, *Rector of Lew Trenchard.*

Lew Trenchard, Devon,
November 10th, 1867.

The Rev. W. HOLDERNESS has undertaken the Sunday duty of this Parish for the year now drawing to a close, and I am happy to testify to the zeal and ability of his Pulpit ministrations, which have been highly acceptable. I believe he would prove, if selected, a valuable Secretary to the British and Foreign Bible Society.

C. BARING GOULD,
Rector of Lew Trenchard.

From the BISHOP OF EXETER.

London, 1st July, 1873.

The Rev. WILLIAM HOLDERNESS was Vicar of Woolfardisworthy West, in the diocese of Exeter, when I came to the diocese, and still holds that office. He has there shown himself a very hard-working, devoted Clergyman, most anxious for the good of his people.

EXETER.

New Testimonials.
The distribution of these manifestoes and testimonials soon quenched the objection that I was a "*foreigner,*" and "*unknown,*" by which we presume the objectors meant that Devon and Dorset were foreign possessions, and that "*unknown*" signified that I was not in the circle of my opponent's personal friends, however "*well known*" to other people.

However, we soon became marvellously "*well known*" in Clerkenwell also, every meeting surpassing its predecessor interest and enthusiasm, until the handful of the first assembly had augmented to such an extent that no room nor any chur in your parish could hold the multitudes of people who strove for admittance.

Then some remark was made concerning the age of the testimonials, and forthwith we published the following new ones, which, with the previous ones, cover our life from boyhood to the present moment.

NEW TESTIMONIALS.

The Deanery, Southampton, July 5th, 1875.

MY DEAR MR. HOLDERNESS,—I wish you all success. I know no one more suited to take up the reins which Mr. Maguire has so long held so faithfully than yourself. Success attend your election.

Faithfully yours,

BASIL WILBERFORCE,
Grandson of the Anti-Slavery Advocate.

The Vicarage, St. Mary's, Hull, July 6th, 1875.

As a native of Hull, Mr. HOLDERNESS has been well and intimately known here for the whole period of his life. He was held in the highest estimation by my late father, the Rev. John Scott, Vicar of St. Mary's, and Lecturer at the Holy Trinity, Hull. Personally blessed under his ministry, Mr. HOLDERNESS was always held in the very warmest affection by my father, who, I know, thought most highly of his qualities and capabilities. Differing somewhat, as I do, from Mr. HOLDERNESS' Church views, my testimony will be, perhaps, the more valuable. I consider him the very man to succeed Mr. Maguire. Genial and hearty in his manner, kind in feeling, and a great softener of asperities, he is well qualified for the difficult post of Vicar of Clerkenwell. An able and most interesting preacher, he is certain to attract and rivet the attention of the masses, by his plain, straightforward, simple language, and at the same time by his quick and ready wit. I have not the slightest hesitation in recommending him heartily to the electors.

JOHN SCOTT, M.A.,
Vicar of St. Mary's, Hull,
Grandson of the Bible Commentator.

Rectory, St. Peter Tavy, Tavistock, 9th July, 1875.

I have known the Rev. W. HOLDERNESS for many years. I deem him to be a very zealous, energetic, and powerful preacher of God's Word, and can testify to the fact that in our neighbourhood his ministry was much valued by a numerous and affectionate people. He seems to have the gift—I will not say the art—of attracting people to God's House, which is a matter of no small importance.

THOMAS GIBBONS,

Rector St. Peter Tavy.

The Rev. WM. HOLDERNESS has been intimately known to me almost from childhood, and we studied together for the sacred office of the ministry, and whilst I regard him as a truly godly and Christian brother, I well know him to be a most zealous clergyman, and a very able and affectionate preacher of Christ's glorious Gospel. He is an earnest and diligent worker, and very ingenious in devising schemes of usefulness. He is physically strong and mentally active, and equal to much exertion. He is warmhearted and genial, and I feel sure would be valued and useful in any parish to which he might be appointed.

CHAS. COOK, D.D.,

Vicar of Holy Trinity, Swansea.

July 9, 1875.

July 10th, 1875.

I have personally known the Rev. W. HOLDERNESS for the last twenty-five years, and I gladly testify to his consistent Christian character, his great activity and usefulness as a clergyman, and his unfailing fidelity to the cardinal truths of the Gospel of Jesus Christ, both in his pastoral work and public ministry.

No man could be further than he from Ritualism; few more devoted to duty; and seldom can a minister of Christ be found possessed of more varied capacities. In the Bible Class, the Lecture Room, or in the open air as a preacher he is at home; and his sermons, whilst sound in doctrine and practical in tendency, are attractive in the highest degree by their force of illustration from science and nature.

Mr. HOLDERNESS is undoubtedly suited to such a parish as Clerkenwell, and in his general, as well as his theological knowledge, he would become not only a faithful preacher amongst the people, but THEIR LEADER IN EVERYTHING THAT WOULD TEND TO ELEVATE OUR COMMON NATURE FROM ITS MANIFOLD DEGRADATIONS.

Mr. HOLDERNESS has so long and so faithfully served in the sacred ministry, that the past of his life, when known to the parishioners of Clerkenwell, cannot fail to be an eloquent witness to his worth ; but I will venture to add this, that by entire reliance upon the Divine blessing, he makes " full proof of his ministry," and his one great object is the salvation of souls.

ROBERT STEPHENSON, M.A.,

Vicar of St. James's, Birkdale, Southport.

Garsdon Rectory, Malmsbury, July 11th, 1875.

MY DEAR SIR,—I have great pleasure in learning that you are a candidate for the Vicarage of Clerkenwell, and hasten to send you a testimonial, which I hope may be of service to you. Without hesitation I affirm, from my pretty long and intimate acquaintance with you, that of all my brother clergymen with whom I am more or less acquainted, and they are very many, you are one of the very fittest men for such a position.

Your ripe age, your activity, your love of work, your good example, your cheerful disposition, your freedom from bigotry and prejudice, your Gospel teaching, and your pulpit power, all proclaim the fact that the electors will do well for themselves, and especially for the poor of Clerkenwell, if they make you their Vicar.

Yours faithfully,

HENRY GALE, D.C.L.,

Rector of Garsdon-in-Lea.

Harpurhey Rectory, Manchester, July 12th, 1875.

I have had the friendship of the Rev. W. HOLDERNESS upwards of thirty years.

For Scriptural faith, force of character, consistency of life wide experience, and power of organisation, the Rev. W. HOLDERNESS is beyond most men.

Having myself had a London parish, the chaplaincy of the Borough Compter, and the chaplaincy of the Lord Mayor, I know something of London requirements, and can say truly that my old friend is a clergyman of the right qualifications.

CHAS. MARSHALL, M.A.,

Rector of Harpurhey.

Clifton Parsonage, July 26th, 1875.

Understanding that the Rev. W. HOLDERNESS is a candidate for the Vicarage of Clerkenwell, I have much pleasure in stating that he was a pupil of my own in his preparation for the ministry. He has since been a very hard-working clergyman in many different spheres—in the Thames Mission, and since that in a parish in the West of England. I would very heartily commend him to the electors of Clerkenwell, and feel sure, that if appointed, he would do his utmost in the large population of Clerkenwell, in preaching the simplicity of the truth as it is in Jesus, and in seeking to gather in souls into the Redeemer's fold.

DAVID ANDERSON, D.D.,

Formerly Bishop of Rupert's Land,

Vicar of Clifton, Chancellor of St. Paul's Cathedral.

St. Mark's Vicarage, Dukinfield, Cheshire, July 20th, 1875.

To the Churchwardens, Vestrymen, and Ratepayers—Electors of the Vicar of Clerkenwell.

GENTLEMEN,—I beg leave to recommend the Rev. WM. HOLDERNESS as just the man to be elected as Vicar of Clerkenwell—a hard-working labourer for the Lord's Vineyard. He has had good experience of parish work and schools. He is a faithful and sound preacher of the Gospel. I heartily wish him success as a candidate for the office of Vicar of Clerkenwell, as I believe he would become acceptable to the people.

I remain, yours faithfully,

WILLIAM HEFFILL.

Windsor, July 20th, 1875.

Having intimately known the Rev. WM. HOLDERNESS for sixteen years, I can bear testimony to his high qualities as a friend, and also his great power as a preacher and lecturer.

DR. SMITH,
Windsor.

RECTOR OF BIDEFORD.

Bideford Rectory, North Devon, July 19th, 1875.

The Rev. W. HOLDERNESS, Vicar of Woolfardisworthy, in this neighbourhood, having offered himself as a candidate for the parish of Clerkenwell, London, I have been requested to give a testimonial as to my knowledge of him as a brother clergyman. I therefore think myself bound to state that I have known him for some years, and for a considerable portion of that time as Sunday Evening Lecturer in my own church. His moral and general character I believe to be perfectly correct.

He is decidedly opposed to all extreme and Ritualistic Church views. He is a man of *more than ordinary energy* in the discharge of his ministerial duties, and would, I should say, be very suitable for such an extensive and poor parish as Clerkenwell.

F. L. BAZELY.
Rector of Bideford.

CHURCHWARDEN OF BIDEFORD.

Bideford, North Devon, 17th July, 1875.

MY DEAR SIR,—In reply to your letter of the 16th inst., I am pleased to hear that you are a candidate for the living of Clerkenwell. I was not aware that you contemplated leaving this neighbourhood, but I can quite understand your preferring a larger field for your labours, and one for which your zeal, energy, and abilities so well qualify you.

Let me add my best hopes that you may be successful, as I am sure, if elected, you would earnestly and faithfully discharge the arduous duties that would devolve upon you.

I am, my dear sir, yours very truly,

ROBERT SIMPKINS, Churchwarden.

The Rev. W. Holderness,
40, Wilmington Square,
Clerkenwell, London.

TESTIMONIALS—*continued.*

CHURCHWARDENS OF WOOLFARDISWORTHY WEST.

"We have heard that the Rev. WILLIAM HOLDERNESS, our esteemed Vicar, is a candidate for the Vicariate of Clerkenwell. The reverend gentleman came here in 1868, and found the church in ruins, and the congregation scattered. By his unwearied activity the church has been almost rebuilt, and a devoted congregation assembled. A new school is about to be built, under the joint management of Churchmen and Dissenters, who unanimously elected Mr. HOLDERNESS to be the chairman of the united board. Nonconformists are drawn to church by his evangelical, interesting, and powerful sermons, and Mr. HOLDERNESS is ever ready to aid them in any good work. In the event of his removal we shall deplore his departure; but we shall be comforted by the reflection that thousands in Clerkenwell will have a faithful pastor and a Gospel preacher, instead of the tens in a scattered rural population. Our prayer is God speed the man, whom the late Baring Gould described as 'The Apostle of the West.'"

(Signed)

GEORGE TURNER,
JOSEPH BURROW,

Churchwardens.

A gentleman connected with an extensive house of business in the parish of Clerkenwell, wandered, in his summer tour, as far as Clovelly and Woolfardisworthy West. From conversations held with my parishioners, he was induced to withdraw from the other side, and to give me his firm support and influence.

This case was not isolated by any means.

That I might not be a stranger to the parishioners, the authorities of the *Daily Chronicle* gave the following short sketch of my life :—

Sketch of Life.
The Rev. William Holderness was born at Kingston-upon-Hull, in 1819. Before he was thirteen years of age he took a leading classical position at the Hull Grammar School; and at this early period of his life he showed unusual aptitude for debating and public speaking. He afterwards pursued his education under Bishop Anderson, now rector of Clifton, and others; and in 1845 he was ordained by the Bishop of Chester, and obtained a curacy at Cockerham. In the next year he was appointed chaplain to the Thames Church Mission, where

His official duties often led him to give farewell services on board emigrant and convict ships. His preaching powers over prisoners, sailors, and others were so well reported to the Home Office, that Lord Palmerston, at the instigation of Sir Joshua Jebb, C.B., gave the head chaplaincy of Portland Convict Establishment to Mr. Holderness, without his having gone through the usual assistant-chaplaincy in the Civil Service. In 1857 Mr. Holderness was transferred to Dartmoor, and here, at the request of the Secretary for the Home Department, he gave to advanced prisoners lectures on scientific subjects, to fit them for colonial life. On leaving the Crown Service, Mr. Holderness accepted the Vicarage of Woolfardisworthy West, near Bideford, Devon, and here he founded a Collegiate School, chiefly for preparing candidates for the ministry. The reverend gentleman is evangelical in his views, and he states that he seeks election to the Vicariate of Clerkenwell, because he would there find a larger sphere for usefulness in ministration and good work.

Lectures and Sermons.

A lecture to children on "The Tabernacle in the Wilderness;" and to adults on "Elocution as shewn at the Bar, the Senate, and the Pulpit;" on "Clocks, Time, and Eternity," &c. &c., on week-evenings; and sermons to the people on the Lord's day have been well attended, and produced good results.

The following report of the probationary sermons is taken from the *Daily Chronicle* of August 10th, 1875:—

ELECTION OF A VICAR FOR CLERKENWELL.

Probationary Sermons by the Rev. Wm. Holderness.

SUNDAY MORNING, AUG. 8.

The Rev. WILLIAM HOLDERNESS, Vicar of Woolfardisworthy West, Devonshire, and one of the candidates for the Vicariate of Clerkenwell, preached two probationary sermons in the parish church on Sunday last. At the morning service the church was crowded to excess, even the reading desk being taken possession of by some tired members of the congregation, and a number of persons were unable to find seats of any kind. The following special hymn was composed by Mr. Holderness for the occasion, and refers to the subject of his discourse, but owing to a mishap of some kind it was not sung:—

THE SONG OF THE ANGELS.

Glory to God, the angels cried,
To see the world's foundations laid ;
With holy joy the heavens rang,
To welcome younger brother—MAN.

Glory to God, the angels sang,
On earth sweet peace, goodwill to man ;
The shepherds heard the joyful strain
When watching flocks on Bethlem's plain.

Glory to God, the angels sing,
When to our Lord we humbly bring
A broken, contrite, lowly heart,
And gladly choose the better part.

Glory to God, again they'll chant
When man is freed from every want ;
When Jesus comes on earth to reign,
Relieving man from woe and pain.

O come, companions in distress,
While travelling in this wilderness ;
With angels sing triumphant songs,
Glory by right to God belongs.

The Rev. Gentleman said: In the second chapter of the Gospel that was written by St. Luke we find it thus recorded in the fourteenth verse—" Glory to God in the highest, and on earth peace, goodwill toward men." In 1788 your fathers engraved this angelic song on a brass plate, covered it with a coat of wax for preservation, and placed it on the foundation stone of this spacious church. From the hour of its concealment no mortal eye has read that grand hymn, and perhaps will not until Jesus shall come with power to complete the work of human redemption, which He commenced in infancy when the heavenly choir rang out the royal anthem, whose chorus was—" Glory to God in the highest, and on earth peace, goodwill toward men." Why did your elders select this passage of Holy Writ from the thousands of apposite and beautiful readings in the Book of Books? Because they wanted the largest amount of sublime truth in the smallest number of words. Herein is manifested the wisdom of their choice; our text contains—engraved as in eternal brass—the epitome of God's designs towards the children of men. Here we have the whole of the Christian system—namely, the exaltation of the

Father's glory, through the salvation of our race by the atonement of the Son. We have the sum and substance of sound religious teaching, as defined by our blessed Lord, when He enjoined that we were to give God the glory, by loving Him with all our heart, soul, and strength, and to promote peace and goodwill amongst men by loving our neighbour as ourselves. Whole libraries of theological volumes have been written; millions of sermons and discourses have been preached, and often has the multitude of words only clouded the clear and simple truth of the Gospel; but the essence of all truth is written on the foundation stone of the temple for the people— His beautiful house of prayer. Your fathers copied it from St. Luke's Gospel; we drag it from its hiding-place to-day, and read the words in your ears again—"Glory to God in the highest, and on earth peace, goodwill toward men." The circumstances under which the words were first sung are remarkable. For four thousand years the world had existed, but certainly not to the due manifestation of God's glory, up to the moment in question. The masses of the human race were sunk into the lowest depths of ignorance, idolatry, and cruelty. Rome held the keys of power both in Church and State. They sold the office of the Jewish high priest annually to the highest bidder; they regarded the world as a field for their arms, and man as an animal to be enslaved or slain in gladiatorial fight for the amusement of their families. They knew neither God nor His glory, as they ought to have done, and what little they understood of the glory of the incorruptible God they changed into an image made like to corruptible man, and to birds, and to four-footed beasts and creeping things; as St. Paul complains in the 25th verse of the first chapter of his letter to these same Romans. The very religion of these proud conquerors brought no glory to Jehovah, for it was a sacerdotal system of iniquity. The most abominable lusts, appetites, and passions were personified, deified, and worshipped under the names of Venus, Bacchus, Diana, and others; their temples were houses of impurity; their priests were servitors of sin and ministers of transgression; their priestesses were, if possible, even worse, and their altars smoked with ignorant bigotry, or blazed out defiantly against the glorious Creator. The work of the people was to cram themselves with luxuries to repletion and to swill themselves into brutal intoxication in festal halls, reclining on couches for the more complete attainment of their swinish purposes. He was the most popular Emperor who caused the largest effusion of blood in the amphitheatre on holidays, which were as far as could be from *holy*days. Bad was the best. Rome at the head of civilisation, yet so base, cruel, and wretched! What must the lower families of the earth have been! So far from living to the honour and glory of God, they were actually existing only to glorify Satan and his train of lusts. If this planet's bad story had closed then, the creation of man would have been a gigantic failure rather than a glory. But in this dark epoch

> " Where was Israel's chosen race ?
> Banished in exile and disgrace."

The ten tribes had been subdued and transported for 725 years, and were yet in hopeless captivity. Judah and Benjamin had been imprisoned for seventy years, and after their release never had again a vigorous, national, or spiritual life. They would not live to God's glory or for man's good, therefore they must be deprived of a liberty and prosperity which they had not the grace to use for the designed purposes of God. When their punitive incarceration in Babylon ceased, like many others they carried the marks of their bondage all their days. They certainly were free—

> " But the splendours of Solomon's reign,
> Never did Judah see again."

The last words of Malachi was "a curse;" then came 400 years of gloomy silence, when no prophet opened his lips, crying— " Comfort ye, comfort ye, my people." Darkness—thick darkness that could be felt—rested upon the inhabitants of the earth like a damp funeral pall. The Church and the world appeared to be dead, and bound in a winding-sheet for burial. The sceptre had departed from Judah, and the lawgiver from between his feet. Ichabod was written on all that once goodly land. The ensign of the House of David no longer was seen on the towers of Jerusalem, but the hated Roman eagle usurped the place of the goodly banner of the shepherd king. The pavement of the holy Temple resounded to the tread of foreign guards and sentinels. Judah's complete humiliation was nigh at hand, even within seventy years—that number of sinister import to her freedom. There is an oppressive stagnation and torpor brooding like a thick cloud over all things, as the darkest period of night is said to be just before the break of day—when hark!—a glad sound is heard—it is the voice of melody singing in angelic strains, as angels only can sing, "Glory to God in the highest, and on earth peace, goodwill toward men." Sing on, ye heavenly host, and join in the chorus, ye children of men, for a new epoch is begun. Darkness was lowering over the people, but God spoke the word,

Let there be light, and light sprang up. Let us look for a moment on those who heard the short sermon and the concluding anthem. The auditors were working men on duty as shepherds, watching their flocks by night. These guardians of the sheep, and more especially of the lambs—the most helpless part of their charge—were hard-working men—persevering, notwithstanding the heat by day and the frost by night, as we learn from Jacob's complaint to his father-in-law, Laban. They required something of the military character and discipline to protect their property from armed robbers, prowling thieves, and wild beasts. Nay, it was sometimes necessary for the good shepherd to lay down his life for the sheep. Why was not the good news made known by the Angel to the High Priest first, or to the Sanhedrim, or to the Bible Clerks, the Scribes, or to some Ecclesiastical authorities, or others? Because these men were not living to the glory of God, nor expecting his kingdom. First in privilege, they were the most loth to take advantage of their high position. Sitting in Moses' seat, they refuse to keep the law, making it of none effect through their tradition—neither entering the kingdom themselves nor allowing the anxious seeker so to do. How history repeats itself; how mournful is the reflection that in the nineteenth century such characters exist in sad abundance! The shepherds were evidently devout men, prayerfully waiting for the consolation of Israel. Those who humbly watch, pray, wait, and seek shall find, and be comforted. To no proud priest or pharisee came the angel announcing the gospel—or good news. The silence of the Temple is unbroken by heavenly voices; but to unlettered working men, that distinguished and powerful open-air preacher cries in the stilly night, "Fear not; for, behold, I bring you good tidings of great joy, which shall be to all people. For unto you is born this day in the city of David a Saviour, which is Christ the Lord. And this shall be a sign to you; Ye shall find the babe wrapped in swaddling clothes, lying in a manger." This brief discourse ended, the field choir of shining ones could be restrained no longer, and they burst into a joyful strain, "Glory to God in the highest, and on earth peace, goodwill toward men" Ah, quibbling scribes and deriding pharisees—ye did not hear that short Gospel sermon, nor did ye thrill with the angelic notes of praise; but the agricultural labourers did. Even so, Father, for so it sometimes pleaseth Thee to hide these things from the wise and prudent and to reveal them unto babes. We grieve to say that in our time there have been men, occupying the highest seats in the Temple, threatening the application of physical force to shepherds crying for bread after watching their flocks by night. The song of songs itself is full of encouraging truth in every letter. Let us more closely examine it. Glory signifies renown, praise, exaltation, and is generally built upon words or deeds or both combined. Thus a man is rendered famous who deviseth something beneficial to the human race, as Peabody, who through his temperate habits was enabled to leave about half a million of money to improve the dwellings of the working men in over-crowded London. For this self-denying act of love to God and man, thousands will glorify God's grace, and call the instrument blessed. All the really glorious deeds of men are founded upon love to God, or they are but as sounding brass or tinkling cymbal, as the 13th chapter of St. Paul's first letter to the Corinthians enforces. Consequently, the true glory of man as an instrument, and the glory of the Almighty as the power and source of glory, are inseparably bound up together, the two cannot be divided. Nothing that injures mankind can possibly bring glory to God or man. Man was created for enduring happiness. When he is happy the end for which he was designed is answered, and his Maker is glorified thereby. When we find him miserable, that is, unhappy, unlike his Creator, then he is so far a mistake, a failure, a spoilt piece of workmanship, bringing no glory to his Divine Fabricator. Had man been made for misery, we could not have thanked the Creator of wretched beings for "creation, preservation, and all the blessings of this life." But, thanks be to God, we can exclaim, ' Get thee hence, loathed melancholy." We were formed for temporal and eternal happiness. The text says so, and the song of the brazen plate repeats the soul-reviving truth. Shout then, ye once desponding but now jubilant people ; break forth into singing—Glory to the highest God, for he sent Jesus Christ to deliver us from the guilt and power of sin, or in other words, to make us truly happy through time and eternity. Blessed be God who moved your fathers to place that gospel tablet as the foundation of the church—glory to God in the highest, through the salvation of men, by Christ the Lord. Blessed are you, their children, if ye attend to what they have written, to the saving of your souls. What foundation for your highest hopes could you have better than that buried brass, which, being dead and buried, yet speaketh. Let it alone. Disturb it not. Other foundation can no man lay than that which is laid, which is Jesus Christ the Righteous. Oh,

"How sweet the name of Jesus sounds
To a believer's ear ! "

This is not the first time that brass has been instrumentally employed to secure the attention and happiness of mortal immortals. Moses made and uplifted a brazen serpent to attract all suffering eyes to the Lamb of God who taketh away the sin of the world, and this was done at the express command of Jehovah. Oh! may the brazen composition which we have uncovered to the eyes of faith this morning lead you now to Christ, the bright and morning star, for it was of His work the angels sang. Those sympathetic elder brethren, ever bright and fair, know how to select and sing words of wisdom better than we poor stammerers of clay. When we meditate on the sacred syllables, and on the sublime scene, we are tempted to forget the decorous usages of this house, and from the pulpit to break forth into singing, "Glory to God in the highest, and on earth peace, goodwill toward men." Come then, brethren, one and all. Cross-examine yourselves before you appear before the bar of God, from whose sentence there is no appeal. Enter into the inmost recesses of your heart and search them with the light of divine truth. Are you living to the glory of God and promoting peace on earth, goodwill to man, as sincere followers of the Prince of Peace? Or are you living for self-glory or vain-glory, or in earnest opposition to Jehovah's praise and man's true welfare? This house was devoted to the

> "Father of all, in every age,
>   In every clime adored,
> By saint, by savage, and by sage,
>   Jehovah, Jove, or Lord."

Are you dedicated to Him as a living temple, showing forth His praise, not only with your lips but with your lives, by giving up yourselves to "His service, and by walking before Him in holiness and righteousness all your days?" It is written, "Whoso offereth praise glorifieth me, and to him that ordereth his conversation aright will I show the salvation of God." Temples built of stone by man's device are valuable, but far more precious are the living temples—human beings, once slaves of sin, snatched as brands from the burning, and transformed into new creatures, by the renewal of the Holy Ghost, through the atonement of Christ Jesus our Lord. To all such the Apostle Paul saith, "Know ye not that your bodies are the temples of the Holy Ghost?" If so, the glory of the Lord should rest upon them and fill them persistently, as it did Solomon's unique structure; and these saved ones should call upon others to partake of their unutterable privileges; until everybody is a splendid temple of the ever blessed God, and according to the promise, "The whole earth is filled with His glory."

SUNDAY EVENING, AUGUST 8TH.

The service in the evening was even better attended than the one in the morning, if possible, for not only was the interior of the church filled to excess, but many persons were unable to obtain admission at all into the building, and had to stand about the door or go away.

The Rev. Gentleman said: In the fifteenth chapter of the Gospel according to St. Luke there is a pathetic story equivalent in pathos to the beautiful history of Joseph in the Old Testament. It is called the history of the Prodigal Son, and is somewhat as follows.

After giving in detail the parable in question, interspersing it with comments, Mr. HOLDERNESS continued: And the young man said, " I will arise and go to my father, and will say unto him, Father, I have sinned against heaven, and before thee, and am no more worthy to be called thy son; make me as one of thy hired servants." You who attend regularly in this house of prayer well know that the resolution of the young man, which we have just read, is one of the introductory sentences used at our morning and evening services. A careless and perfunctory clergyman, who had recited these words for many years, without due thoughtfulness, was one morning impelled to question himself gravely after uttering them. Much alarmed, he mentally demanded—O my soul, hast thou ever really arisen and gone to thy Father? The incident was the turning point in his existence, the germ of new life in his soul. Let us pray that this night may witness a repetition of the miracle of grace in many hearts, and that not a few may actually arise, go to their heavenly Father, and tell him all their pent-up grief, and soon rejoice in conscious pardon and peace, which is a privilege belonging to the truly penitent, through godly sorrow for sin. The scope of the whole pathetic story was to teach the exceeding great love of the Father for all His children, and to rebuke the selfish spirit of the Jew, which Christ foresaw he would entertain towards his Gentile brother. These are the two great leading outlines of instruction embracing minor lessons suitable for every age, rank, and country to the end of time. For the sake of retention by the memory they might be considered in the following order:—1st, a morbid love of independence, coupled with a hatred of control and responsibility. Let us not err on this subject. It is a just and proper feeling for a youth to long for the time when he will no longer be burdensome to his industrious parents. His training and education are to give him the power to earn his own bread by the sweat of his brow or brains, and in due time to be prepared for the headship of his own house and home. This is a highly commendable love of independence. Very different ideas possessed the younger son when he said, " Father, give me now the property I might expect at your death, and let me go from under your inspection and roof to spend my fortune as I list in following the devices and desires of my own heart without let or hindrance, or any one to say, What doest thou?" This is a most unwholesome love of independence, invariably leading to condign punishment and grief. The morbid desire began in the garden of Eden, and is intensified, rather than worn out, in the latter part of the nineteenth century. Our first parents would not brook the salutary restriction even from a tree which was hurtful to them. What to them were the tens of thousands delicious fruits graciously provided for delectable food so long as there was one tree which they might not touch! That one reserved shrub, in their estimation, deprived all the rest of beauty and delight. We, the fallen offspring of rebellious parents, are afflicted with similar vices, strengthened with nearly six thousand years of experiment. In inexperienced youth, more especially, how soon is impatient waywardness displayed. We want to go out and come in when we desire, by night and by day, resenting any inquiry as to where we have been, how employed, and what company we had in our pursuits. Young persons of both sexes have the haziest views of the first commandment with promise, even if they can repeat it properly. They too often sigh after unlimited hours, money, and appliances for hunting unattainable pleasures. The young man in question had an excellent home and father, who appeared to have studied nothing more than the welfare of his children. Here let me observe that it is the bounden duty of parents to make the home circle the brightest and happiest spot on earth, that their sons may not be induced to forsake their father's house, as gloomy, in search of pleasure elsewhere. Yet, notwithstanding all his home comforts, he impudently demands his share of the parental property to be immediately given to him. Imagine our feelings in the event of our younger son, or any son, saying, "Father, give me at once the property I might expect at your death." By virtue of an old Gentoo law, existing in the days of our Lord, a youth might prefer such a claim if he were cruelly used by his father; and should the father be able to prove that he had never given his boy any ground for complaint, the magistrate might inflict a heavy fine on the offender. This law, no doubt, was well known to the young man, therefore he gathered all his substance together, and took his departure into a distant land, where he might be hidden from the claims of justice, and make his fortune so unpalpable that no fine could be levied thereon. He selected apparently a temporary abode among a thriftless people, who quickly helped him to squander his belongings, for amongst these vicious characters he wasted his substance with a spendthrift's spending, that is, with most culpable extravagance. From the elder brother's complaint we ascertain the worthlessness and profligacy of his associates. Such companionship leads straight to misery. Can any man sow thistles and hope to reap wheat? All animals except men—the lords of creation—seek their own good; but man was damaged in his intellect by the fall; hence we find him pursuing the most idiotic devices to find happiness or its synonym—pleasure—and securing nothing but misery and wretchedness. Who ever saw a sheep try to slake its thirst at a sandhill? But the poor fool known as man goes to more unlikely places and pursuits in a vain endeavour to meet the cravings of his soul for happiness. Colonel Gardner relates that when he was considered by his gay military companions to be one of the most handsome and highly-favoured uniformed officers of his day, he has seen a dog enter the mess-room prowling for food, and looked at the creature with envy, inwardly groaning and exclaiming, "Oh, that I were that dog!" Since his time thousands have felt the same iron enter their souls, although looked upon by their comrades as men enjoying life in rich abundance. The spendthrift's spending, as the words should be rendered, did not last long. Young men of this mental calibre could soon finish the 750 millions of the national debt, and more, if they only had possession. They have only to bet and gamble for higher stakes, and parks and farms and ships and houses will vanish, like a dissolving view, into poverty, disease, wretchedness, and death. Anxious parents may rush to the rescue sometimes, but at last they grow weary, hopeless, and powerless, and turn their pale faces, with broken hearts, to the wall, murmuring as they die, "Ephraim is joined to his idols, let him alone. I loved that boy as I loved my life; I would have died to effectually serve him, but he preferred any society to mine, wallowed in iniquity, and has brought down my grey hairs with sorrow to the grave." Those who have watched the insect world have never observed the industrious bees or provident ants squander their stores as silly mortals do and call the operation "enjoying life." Can folly any further go? Go to the ant, thou sluggard—prodigal of time, God's precious gift to man—consider her ways and be wise. Birds, beasts, fishes, insects, and reptiles, though lower in the social scale than we, yet in many points are much wiser, and set us bright examples which the Scriptures bid us copy. Now the scene is changed, the goods are wasted; those who helped to consume them are fled as rate forsake a doomed ship. Plenty of companions, male and females can the young man have so long as his money lasts, but no longer. The prodigals of railway and Crystal Palace notoriety had crowded tables until the firm hand of Justice was on their shoulders to arrest them in their mad career. Be sure your sin will find you out, as the bloodhound tracks the dusky slave in the dismal swamp. Do I speak to any this night living in known sin? Give it up, my brother, at once and for ever, before it explodes into public notice and comes under magisterial authority—too late for forgiveness or restitution. Just where you sit resolve to surrender, and when you go home put that resolution into practice. I know not why I am so strongly moved this night thus to speak, but your conscience at this moment may be telling you, "This is a message from God unto me." Hunger is a sharp thorn. "He began to be in want, and no man gave unto him." What? Where were those who had feasted at his expense and to his ruin, eating and drinking his very financial vitality to death? Could they not give him at least some plain, cheap food, and advice, more cheap? No, not they. Not a crumb of comfort, not a cup of cold water, did they bestow upon their quondam patron who so lately fed them, alas, too sumptuously. Ah me! The convivial friendship of the young or old worldling is the most bitter mockery of the holy word "friendship" that can be conceived. His false friends loved not him, but his viands and costly dishes. Necessity has no law. Something must immediately be done. It is of no use to beg if none will give. Man was sentenced to win his bread by toil, and the late youth of fashion must work or starve. Alas! What can the exquisite do that he may eat a morsel of bread? What are numbers of our extravagant young men to do when the resources of the frugal are dried up, when the gatherings of their fathers are gone? If there was one calling more horrible to a wealthy young Jew than another, it was that of feeding swine, which was to him an unclean animal; and the occupation was also laborious, from the quantity of bulky food required. Princes and law-givers have tended sheep, but the swineherd was the lowest slave amongst Jews and Saxons. This deep degradation might have been endured if his bucolic master had allowed him a sufficiency of coarse, unwholesome human food, but this boon and right were denied him. No man gave unto him; therefore he must sustain his animal life with swine's food; he must serve the pigs, and contend with them for a morsel of sustentation to keep the spark of life alive. How are the mighty fallen! Plantagenets have been found keeping a toll-gate, prodigals feeding swine. It is just and meet that those who manifest less wisdom than animals should be brought lower than the vilest brutes. But now he is coming to himself, to use the Scriptural expression. He begins to think. There is some hope when a man begins to think, and no longer "whistles as he goes for want of thought." The sinner's course won't bear calm reflection. Then he hears the voice of love and mercy saying, "Come now, let us reason together, though your sins be as scarlet they shall be white as snow." Reflection led to resolve, and resolve to action. Had he been contented by simply saying, Yes, I certainly will—some day—arise and go to my father, he might have perished in his transgression, as he who said, "Go thy way for this time; when I have a convenient season I will call for thee." Oh, my people, do you not perceive that the portrait we have been contemplating is a photograph of each person in this house to-night, with the difference that some of us, it may be, have not come to ourselves—never perhaps seriously reflected on their soul's prosperity for one single consecutive half-hour? Come, then, come to the Saviour; no more delay. Arise and go to your Father; tell Him all about your sins, sufferings and misery, and He will run to meet you with open arms. I knew a youth of nineteen years who thought he had no need of a Saviour, so long as he kept from criminal acts, attended church twice on Sundays, and came to the Lord's Table—well, not very often. But it pleased God to show him, about that time, that he must be born again, or die to all eternity—that he and all men as much need conscious conversion as Nero, Caligula, or any of the Popes. He had no rest until he individually came to the Saviour, and found pardon and peace through believing. He rose and went to his Father and was comforted. Shortly afterwards he was called to declare the Gospel message to perishing sinners, telling every one with whom he came into contact what a glorious Saviour he had found, and causing many, instrumentally, to turn and live. Arise, then, and come to your Father. There is bread enough and to spare. Come, then, and tell Him your heart's desire, and He will save you with an everlasting salvation.

In addition to these two sermons, lessons for the day, and full services, we were pleased to be allowed the privilege of conducting the prayer meeting at the Sunday School, and giving short Scriptural expositions to a very crowded assembly.

Amongst other literary productions evoked by the contest, the following have appeared, by which numerous gentlemen have shown their interest, the following appeal, in consequence of Mr. Rose's retirement, and also the circulation of sundry bills, has been contributed :—

Reasons why the Rev. WILLIAM HOLDERNESS *ought to become Vicar of Clerkenwell.*

BECAUSE the Poor Man's Church should be made attractive to the Poor Man. It can only become so by popular and sympathetic preaching, in which qualification the Rev. WM. HOLDERNESS exceptionally excels. Well-wishers of the Church should, therefore, cheerfully accord him their suffrages.

BECAUSE it is desirable the Vicar should not alone be a qualified preacher, but a man also able to follow, instruct, and, if need be, lecture upon scientific and secular subjects. The Rev. WM. HOLDERNESS' proved educational power, his erudition, and ability to communicate the information he possesses to others, mark him as eminently fitted to obtain the attention and confidence of an artisan population. It is, therefore, the duty of those who insist upon a wide and liberal education for the masses, to see that he is elected.

BECAUSE the popular plaint of all Denominations (and particularly that of the Established Church) is the indifference of the Working Classes to religion; this has its origin in the lack of sympathy between the Clergy and the People. The Rev. WM. HOLDERNESS enters into the hopes and aspirations of all classes of the community, and is essentially capable of drawing towards his ministry the lower orders; upholders of Town Missions should therefore support his election to the Parish Pulpit.

BECAUSE, in these times of covert Papacy, the great need of the nation is an open, pronounced, Evangelical utterance, from the Clergy, in defence of private conscience. The Rev. WM. HOLDERNESS is an eloquent exponent and defender of Evangelical as opposed to High Church views; it therefore the paramount duty of Protestants to vote for him.

BECAUSE one heavy stumbling-block to be overcome in the path of Christian effort is the needless barriers separating believers into Sects. The Rev. WM. HOLDERNESS' broad sympathies and most cherished aspirations lead him to seek and accept, in our Saviour's service, the co-operation of all our Nonconforming brethren ; the faithful, therefore, of every Denomination should esteem it a privilege to secure his success.

UPHOLDERS OF THE REFORMATION, is it your desire to maintain Grand Old Luther's right of private judgment, for which your forefathers suffered ? because, if so, you must help the Election of the Rev. WM. HOLDERNESS, who firmly puts his foot upon new-fangled Romish projects.

MEMBERS OF THE CHURCH OF ENGLAND, is it your sincere desire to see the old Mother Church retain her hold on the People ? if so, it is your business to place those in its ministration who can fill the walls of its edifices ; can elicit self-support from its attendant congregations, and keep it clear from liabilities. Do you wish this for the Parish Church of Clerkenwell ? if so, vote for the Rev. WM. HOLDERNESS.

SABBATH SCHOOL TEACHERS, is it your hope to secure a loving Superintendent of your devoted labours, who understands your onerous and self-sacrificial duties, who can engage the attention of Children and Youths, and assist them in the way they should go ? if so, help to elect the Rev. WM. HOLDERNESS, who has proved his capacity in that walk of life.

RATEPAYERS, your Vicar, whoever he may be, is an ex-officio Member of your Vestry. Is it your hope to have your burdens of local taxation lessened, or efficiency for its outlay secured ? if so, elect one who can and will take his fair share in supervision of the local needs and expenditure of your Parish.

FELLOW PARISHIONERS OF CLERKENWELL! for the above and other cogent reasons, I hold it the bounden duty of Electors of every class in our Parish to Poll at the ensuing Election for the Rev. WM. HOLDERNESS, and secure his great administrative talent for this Parish.

Yours,

A CHURCHMAN.

Now, ladies and gentlemen, our case is complete. You have heard the testimony of a cloud of witnesses. You have beheld the eagerness of the people in pressing to hear the Word of God. One man, in gratitude, wrung my hand, saying, with emotion, "*You have taught me more of the Bible in one hour than I had learned in my previous life.*" You have seen how interestingly children can be taught by objective teaching, and youths by technical instruction. Without fear, favour, or affection, prayerfully consider your determination, remembering St. Luke's description of a somewhat similar deliberation at Jerusalem, as read in the 1st chapter of the Acts of the Apostles, the 24th verse: "*And they prayed and said, Thou, Lord, which knowest the hearts of all men, shew which of these two thou hast chosen.*"

Summing up.

I am, Ladies and Gentlemen,

Your obedient servant,

WM. HOLDERNESS,

Vicar of Woolfardisworthy West, near Bideford.

PRINTED BY CASSELL PETTER AND GALPIN, LUDGATE HILL, LONDON, E.C.

ERRATUM.

In the hurry of printing an unfortunate omission has occurred: on page 29, line 6, after "Mr. Rose's retirement," please add "*from the platform.*"

www.ingramcontent.com/pod-product-compliance
Lightning Source LLC
Chambersburg PA
CBHW081306040426
42452CB00014B/2677